Dynamic Drag Racers

by Michael Sandler

Consultant: Mike McNessor
Automotive Journalist

BEARPORT
PUBLISHING

New York, New York

Credits

Cover and Title Page, © se4/ZUMA Press/Newscom; 4–5, © Chris Szagola/CSM/Landov; 6T, © Chris Szagola/CSM/Landov; 6B, © AP Images/NHRA/Auto Imagery, Inc.; 7T, © Michael Dinovo/CSM/Landov; 7B, © Jose Carlos Fajardo/MCT/Landov; 8, © 2010 autoimagery.com; 8-9, © 2010 autoimagery.com; 10, © 2010 autoimagery.com; 11, © AP Images/Gainesville Sun/Brad McClenny; 12, © Joan Adlen/Hulton Archive/Getty Images; 13, © Chris Putman/Icon SMI/Newscom; 14, © 2010 autoimagery.com; 14–15, © 2010 autoimagery.com; 16, © 2010 autoimagery.com; 17, © 2010 autoimagery.com; 18, Courtesy of Bill "Maverick" Golden; 19, Courtesy of Bill "Maverick" Golden; 20, © Jose Carlos Fajardo/Contra Costa Times/MCT/Newscom; 21, © Chris Szagola/Cal Sport Media/Newscom; 22T, © Mark Tolerico; 22B, © 2010 autoimagery.com.

Publisher: Kenn Goin
Senior Editor: Lisa Wiseman
Creative Director: Spencer Brinker
Design: Debrah Kaiser
Photo Researcher: Picture Perfect Professionals, LLC

Library of Congress Cataloging-in-Publication Data

Sandler, Michael, 1965–
 Dynamic drag racers / by Michael Sandler.
     p. cm. — (Fast rides)
 Includes bibliographical references and index.
 ISBN-13: 978-1-61772-138-0 (library binding)
 ISBN-10: 1-61772-138-7 (library binding)
 1. Dragsters—Juvenile literature. 2. Drag racers—Juvenile literature. I. Title.
 TL236.2.S26 2011
 796.72—dc22

                              2010041872

For more information, write to Bearport Publishing Company, Inc., 101 Fifth Avenue, Suite 6R, New York, New York 10003. Printed in the United States of America in North Mankato, Minnesota.

122010
10810CGD

10 9 8 7 6 5 4 3 2 1

Table of CONTENTS

Drag Racing

Drag racing is the simplest motor sport around. Two vehicles line up. The green starting light flashes. The drivers then take off and race to the finish line.

Races last only a few seconds. That's because the race is usually just a quarter mile (402 m) long or, for the most powerful racers, a 1,000-foot (305-m) **run**. Yet over these short distances, blazing engines push drag cars or motorcycles to incredible speeds. There is no doubt—drag racing is the fastest sport in the world!

Two cars at the start of a drag race

In this book, you'll learn all about the different types of drag racing vehicles and the drivers who are brave enough to race them. So fasten your seat belt and get ready for the ride of a lifetime.

Drag Racers

There are many types of drag racers. Four of the most popular ones today are Pro Stock cars, Pro Stock motorcycles, Funny Cars, and **Top Fuel dragsters**.

Pro Stock racers look somewhat like ordinary "stock" cars—everyday cars that anyone can buy. Looks are deceiving, however. Beneath the hoods of these cars are racing engines with special parts that allow them to reach speeds of more than 200 miles per hour (322 kph). Almost as fast, Pro Stock motorcycles are **custom built** machines that are specially designed for drag racing.

A Pro Stock car

A Pro Stock motorcycle

Faster than Pro Stock cars are both Funny Cars and Top Fuel dragsters. Funny Cars, which are named for their "funny-looking" stretched-out bodies, can reach speeds of 315 miles per hour (507 kph) or more. Long, sleek Top Fuel dragsters are the fastest drag racers of all. Some can speed down a drag strip at around 330 miles per hour (531 kph). They go so fast that they rely on body parts called **wings** to keep their tires from lifting off the track.

A Funny Car

wing

A Top Fuel dragster

Pro Stock cars and motorcycles run on **racing gas**. Funny Cars and Top Fuel dragsters use a special fuel mix made up mainly of **nitro**, which helps these cars go superfast.

Penhall/Young Life Pontiac GXP

TYPE: Pro Stock car   **DRIVER:** Mike Edwards
TOP SPEED: 212.03 miles per hour (341.23 kph)
TRACK: Houston Raceway Park, Baytown, Texas

Most drivers get a sinking feeling when they find out they're racing against Mike Edwards. Mike, the 2009 **NHRA** Pro Stock champion, drives a monster Pro Stock car. In March 2009, his red-and-white Pontiac GXP became the first Pro Stock car to top 212 miles per hour (341 kph) in a race.

Mike Edwards after winning a competition in 2010

wheelie bars

Mike Edwards's Pontiac GXP

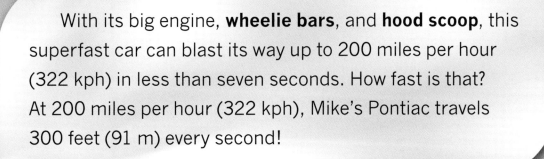

With its big engine, **wheelie bars**, and **hood scoop**, this superfast car can blast its way up to 200 miles per hour (322 kph) in less than seven seconds. How fast is that? At 200 miles per hour (322 kph), Mike's Pontiac travels 300 feet (91 m) every second!

Pro Stock cars use special racing engines that can cost more than $175,000 each. They produce about 1,300 **horsepower** and burn through gas at 7.5 gallons (28 l) a minute. An everyday car might have around 200 horsepower and run for three hours on the same amount of gas.

hood scoop

Castrol GTX Ford Mustang

TYPE: Funny Car **DRIVER:** Ashley Force Hood
TOP SPEED: 316.38 miles per hour (509.16 kph)
TRACK: zMax Dragway, Concord, North Carolina

Like other Funny Cars, Ashley Force Hood's Castrol GTX Ford Mustang has a monstrously powerful engine. When pushed as hard as it can go, her car uses fuel at about the same rate as a 747 jet plane. The car's **wheelbase** is long, with huge tires in back and skinny ones in front. On the roof, there's an escape hatch just in case of an accident.

Ashley grew up around Funny Cars. Her father, John Force, is a drag racing legend who won 14 Funny Car championships. Although Ashley doesn't have as many trophies as her dad, she still has many accomplishments to be proud of. For example, in March 2010, Ashley's Ford reached an amazing 316.38 miles per hour (509.16 kph), setting the national Funny Car speed record for a 1,000-foot (305-m) run.

Ashley Force Hood

Funny Cars like Ashley's Mustang go so fast that they can't just rely on brakes to stop. Two parachutes pop out of the back to slow down the car once it passes the finish line.

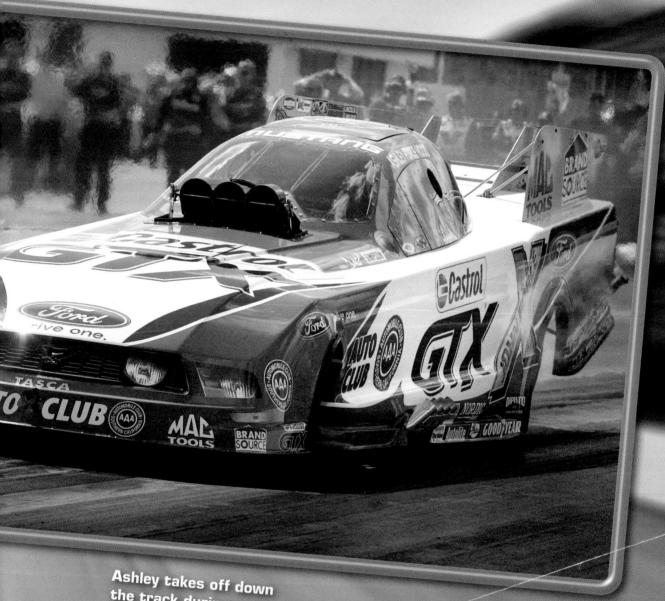

Ashley takes off down the track during a race in Gainesville, Florida, in 2010.

Swamp Rat

TYPE: Top Fuel   **DRIVER:** Don Garlits
TOP SPEED: 323.04 miles per hour (519.88 kph)
TRACK: Gainesville Raceway, Gainesville, Florida

Top Fuel cars are drag racing's fastest and most powerful vehicles. They owe their modern rear engine design to the most famous drag racer in history—"Big Daddy" Don Garlits. Don won 17 Top Fuel championships in cars that he called Swamp Rats. Through the 1960s, he built his Swamp Rat dragsters like everyone else—with the engine in front of the driver.

Don Garlits and Swamp Rat 30 in 1987

Unfortunately, these cars weren't very safe. If the engines blew up, which they sometimes did, parts and flames could fly back and injure the driver. In 1970, this happened to "Big Daddy" during a California race and he was badly hurt. To keep this from happening again, Don designed a safer Swamp Rat with the engine in the back. Today, all Top Fuel dragsters are made this way.

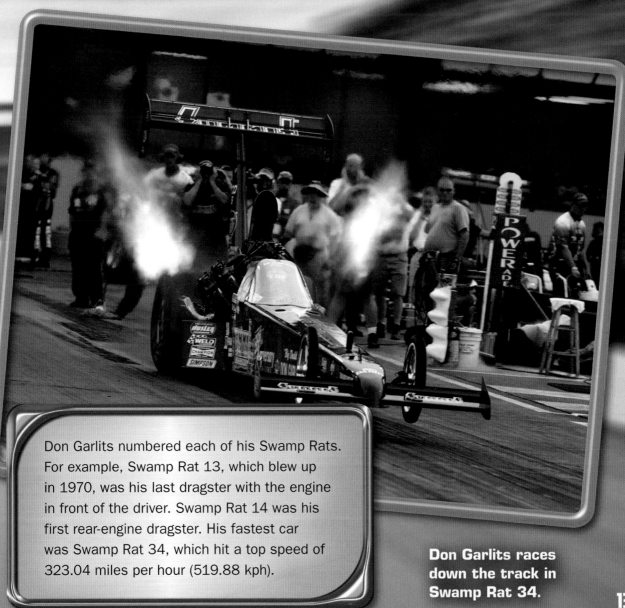

Don Garlits numbered each of his Swamp Rats. For example, Swamp Rat 13, which blew up in 1970, was his last dragster with the engine in front of the driver. Swamp Rat 14 was his first rear-engine dragster. His fastest car was Swamp Rat 34, which hit a top speed of 323.04 miles per hour (519.88 kph).

Don Garlits races down the track in Swamp Rat 34.

Screamin' Eagle
Harley-Davidson V-Rod

TYPE: Pro Stock motorcycle   **DRIVER:** Andrew Hines
TOP SPEED: 197.45 miles per hour (317.76 kph)
TRACK: Gainesville Raceway, Gainesville, Florida

Like other Pro Stock motorcycles, Andrew Hines's Harley is different from bikes that people buy for everyday use. How? It has super-light **carbon fiber** body panels that help smooth the flow of air around the bike and increase the motorcycle's speed. The engine runs on racing fuel instead of ordinary gas. The rear tire is extra wide, so more rubber touches the track, giving the bike gripping power and helping it to speed up quickly. A wheelie bar in back keeps the bike from flipping over.

Andrew Hines poses with his trophy after winning a competition.

While riding his Harley, Andrew has become a three-time Pro Stock motorcycle champion. In 2005, he set a Pro Stock motorcycle speed record when his bike reached 197.45 miles per hour (317.76 kph) in a Gainesville, Florida, race.

At age 21, Andrew became the youngest world champion in NHRA history.

Andrew Hines roars down the track on his Harley.

Racers Edge Suzuki

TYPE: Pro Stock motorcycle   **DRIVER:** Michael Phillips
TOP SPEED: 197.65 miles per hour (318.08 kph)
TRACK: Infineon Raceway, Sonoma, CA

When Michael Phillips was just 13 years old, he got his first motorcycle. He started racing right away, even though he wasn't tall enough to get on the bike by himself.

Since then, Michael has gotten bigger—and so have the bikes he rides. Today he rides the super-quick Racers Edge Suzuki. In July 2010, Michael and his bike broke Andrew Hines's record and became the fastest motorcycle team in the world. They roared across the finish line at 197.65 miles per hour (318.08 kph) in the **semifinals** of an NHRA competition in Sonoma, California.

Setting the motorcycle speed record was great, but Michael wanted something more—a win in the 2010 NHRA finals against Andrew Hines. He got that win by beating Andrew and his Harley by barely a fiftieth of a second.

Michael Phillips holds up his trophy at the 2010 NHRA competition.

Michael Phillips riding his Racers Edge Suzuki

Little Red Wagon

TYPE: Show Car/Wheelstander   **DRIVER:** Bill "Maverick" Golden
TOP TRICK: A record 4,230-foot (1,289-m) wheelstand

While it may not be a Funny Car or a Pro Stock car, the Little Red Wagon is certainly one of the most famous drag racers around. This **exhibition dragster** is known for doing tricks rather than racing. The wagon began life as a 1965 Dodge pickup. Then, its small **factory engine** was removed. A huge, **modified** Chrysler **Hemi** was mounted in the rear of the truck, turning it into a dragster. The first time Bill Golden drove the truck in 1965, the front wheels launched up toward the sky as the Hemi kicked in. The Little Red Wagon zoomed down the racetrack, popping a wheelie at more than 100 miles per hour (161 kph).

Bill and his **wheelstander** became famous for this trick. For more than three decades, the Little Red Wagon thrilled drag racing fans by screaming from the starting line on two wheels with its **tailgate** dragging on the ground and sparks flying in the air.

Bill Golden and the Little Red Wagon

In 1977, the Little Red Wagon made history by popping a 4,230-foot-long (1,289-m) wheelie. That wheelie put Bill and the Little Red Wagon into *The Guinness Book of World Records*.

U.S. Army Dragster

TYPE: Top Fuel **DRIVER:** Tony Schumacher
TOP SPEED: 337.58 miles per hour (543.28 kph)
TRACK: Brainerd International Raceway, Brainerd, Minnesota

What's today's top Top Fuel racer? It's Tony Schumacher's U.S. Army dragster. This car weighs in at around 2,225 pounds (1,009 kg). That's extremely light for a vehicle that's about twice as long as an ordinary car and has a massive aluminum engine. The 8,000-horsepower Chrysler Hemi engine can power the car to 100 miles per hour (161 kph) in less than one second.

Tony Schumacher celebrates after winning a race in 2007.

In 2005, the U.S. Army dragster became the fastest Top Fueler in the world when it reached 337.58 miles per hour (543.28 kph) in a quarter-mile (402-m) run. From 2004 to 2009, Tony won six Top Fuel championships while driving this car.

Tony and the U.S. Army dragster during a race in 2009

Tony's car, like other Top Fuel dragsters, **accelerates** more quickly than any other type of land vehicle and at least one space vehicle—the Space Shuttle!

More Dynamic Drag Racers

The Cool Bus

Who says school buses can't be cool? The 20-foot-long (6-m) Cool Bus is a drag racing show truck with a 1,000-horsepower engine. It may be the longest wheelstander in the world.

Shirley Muldowney's Top Fuel Dragster

Shirley Muldowney, the first woman ever to drive a Top Fuel dragster and the first person to win two Top Fuel championships, drove just about every type of drag racer during her career. Here, Shirley is spinning the rear tires of her Top Fuel dragster, heating them up in preparation for a run.

GLOSSARY

accelerates (ak-SEL-uh-*rates*) speeds up

carbon fiber (KAR-bun FYE-bur) a material made from thin carbon threads that is very strong but also very light

custom built (KUHSS-tuhm BILT) made from scratch

exhibition dragster (ek-suh-BISH-uhn DRAG-stur) a dragster primarily used as a show car

factory engine (FAK-tuh-ree EN-juhn) the engine that was put into a vehicle when it was first made

Hemi (HEM-ee) a powerful auto engine first built by the Chrysler Corporation

hood scoop (HOOD SKOOP) a raised scoop-shaped part on the hood of a car that improves airflow to the engine

horsepower (HORSS-pou-ur) one measure of an engine's power

modified (MOD-uh-fyed) changed or improved

NHRA (EN-AYCH-AR-AYE) stands for the National Hot Rod Association; this group organizes and sets the rules for the most important American drag races

nitro (NYE-troh) short for nitromethane; a special racing fuel used by some drag racing cars

racing gas (RAYSS-ing GASS) a high-performance fuel mix used by racing cars

run (RUHN) a single trip down a drag strip

semifinals (SEM-ee-*fye*-nuhlz) the next-to-last round in a competition

tailgate (TALE-*gayt*) the board at the back of a truck that can be folded down or removed for loading and unloading things

Top Fuel dragsters (TOP FYOO-uhl DRAG-sturz) nitro-fueled rear-engine cars that are the fastest type of drag racers

wheelbase (WEEL-bayss) the distance between the center of the front wheels and the center of the back wheels in an automobile

wheelie bars (WEEL-ee BARZ) bars with small wheels attached to the back of a car or a motorcycle; these bars keep the vehicle's front wheels from lifting up too high in the air

wheelstander (WEEL-stand-ur) a car or truck that can lift its front wheels into the air and drive with only its rear wheels on the ground

wings (WINGZ) body parts on the backs of Top Fuel dragsters that put a downward force on the cars and keep the tires pressing down on the track

Bibliography

Miller, Timothy. *Drag Racing: The World's Fastest Sport*. Buffalo, NY: Firefly Books (2009).

Car and Driver Magazine

espn.com

nhra.com

Read More

Gigliotti, Jim. *Hottest Dragsters and Funny Cars (Wild Wheels!)*. Berkeley Heights, NJ: Enslow (2008).

McCollum, Sean. *Dragsters (Full Throttle)*. Mankato, MN: Capstone (2010).

Zuehlke, Jeffrey. *Drag Racers (Motor Mania)*. Minneapolis, MN: Lerner (2008).

Learn More Online

To learn more about drag racers, visit
www.bearportpublishing.com/FastRides

Index

About the Author

Brooklyn-based writer Michael Sandler has written numerous books about sports, from drag racing to football, for kids and teens.